Between My Thoughts

Betty Kituyi Mukhalu

Smallberry Press

Copyright © 2017 Betty Kituyi Mukhalu
All rights reserved.

The right of Betty Kituyi Mukhalu to be identified as the author of this work has been asserted by her in accordance with the Copyright, Designs and Patents Act 1988.

No text of this publication may be reproduced, copied or transmitted except with written permission or in accordance with the provisions of the Copyright Act 1956 (as amended). Any person who does any unauthorised act in relation to this publication may be liable to criminal prosecution and civil claims for damages.

A CIP catalogue record of this book is available from the British Library. ISBN: 978-0-9930315-3-3

Published by Smallberry Press, International House, 24 Holborn Viaduct, London EC1A 2BN. www.smallberrypress.co.uk

Front cover image copyright Tanom Kongchan/Shutterstock.com

CONTENTS

July	1
Cacti	2
Destroying a woman's fragrance	3
Broken dreams	4
The Circle	6
Falling Stars	7
What is that?	8
Hibiscus	10
To a daughter	11
Pick-pocket stranger	12
Third Word Champion	13
The Vase	14
A Dark Night	15
Celebration	17
Shoreline	19
Hanging Threads	20
A Poem on a Bus	22

My child sees	24
Cooking for a son	25
Acorn of my tree	26
My Coma Tale	27
A Fertile Desert	28
Higenyi	29
A Sketch	31
A Bee-kissed Garden	32
Something vulnerable	33
Spider	35
Candle	36
Meeting as Spirit	37
My flower's path	38
Little Edens	39
Falling	40

July

July moon stands
too far for company;
with no one to meet,
encounter is free of presence.

This dwelling
is a haunted jungle:
wild and desolate,
deserted of all loveliness.

Cacti

My favourite,
starting to blossom;
I can't wait to see their flower,
I have never seen one before.

The black and grey spots
in the foreground are
their flowers coming out.

Destroying a woman's fragrance

As she extends a hand
to her nearest neighbour,
a woman destroys all that is
artificial in her.

Yet inside her home,
there are holes that drain
her oil, abduct her fragrance
in a moment of fury.

It is the act of destroying
a woman's fragrance
that is unforgivable
amongst the noblest of saints.

Broken dreams

"People who live in small crowded places have broken dreams" – Monica Arach

This Saturday
my dreams lie in balance, but
the ground is shaking;
it is hard to stand in one place.

The tables are flying,
the sugar bowls
are thrown broken;
I am the one to collect
the broken pieces
and keep them safely
away where they
will not cut our feet.

Although on the surface
dreams seem broken
into pieces, I remain
untouched and unbroken.

I have to live this dream

for both of us, yes   this dream
is possible on the inside of me.

The Circle

The circle meanders;
a loop of silver glinting,
a hoop of steel:
piercing women, young and old.

A circle of suffering
whose victims stand straight:
soldiers of little things
feeding a mouth,
comforting with a
patting hand;

they stand strong,
sharing pain
in the circle's
burnished gleam.

Falling Stars

Heavy clouds born
of lightning and thunder
from the lovers' throats:
they are surging through
the skyline.

Stars have surrendered their lustre,
falling in the eyes of sisters,
rolling into rivers of sorrow,
flowing freely, washing.

In the sisters' eyes,
the stars shine;
in the rainbow of their tears
the sisters are one.

What is that?

What is that
in the space
between my thoughts
when I look with my eyes?

Are they silent whispers
waiting to be heard,
or invisible codes
hiding to be deciphered?

Is it the goldenness
in the landscape,
a mist of certainty or
a sublime beauty
slipping under my feet?

What is that
in the slow step I take,
which causes me to notice?

Could it be
a passing visitation
of euphoria or the ecstasy

that comes with feeling whole?

Could it be passing circles
of destiny, which wrap around
those who walk
quietly on the land?

Does my mind play with me
or do I see a beloved in a man?

But do I see it or do I become
a deity that happens to be
between two strides?

Is this what others call
a window of one's soul?

Whatever that is,
I see it under the bridge;
I am here, I am there,
between my thoughts,
between this distance.

Hibiscus

The red flower on my pillow
smiles, blinks, whispers
karibuni* Jadin.

The floor was mopped, this bed
was made; I am buoyed by the strength
of my caring hands, enveloped in the
warmth of the moment, charmed
by the language of the hibiscus.

The ocean swims, the wind sighs;
my eyes catch the drizzle of sleep,
my heart sweeps   into the unknown.

*Karibuni – Kiswahili word for welcome.

To a daughter

A mother is
a sister in knowing
the unexplained;
a star in the garden
of their home.

She who practices
grandmother's wisdom, brings
a whole nation into being.

Pick-pocket stranger

To the young man in a gang
by the corner:

your blood-stained eyes,
petrol scented breath,
dirty swift feet
haunt my mind's eye.

I wonder if you gaze
in the fire nightlong
or cross a stream.

Like a hungry bee
from a hive
you sting women's throats,
grab their gold,
rip their hearts.

At a distance
you watch   a mother
perplexed, terrified
at the child she bore: you
have become a stranger.

Third World Champion

His race begins in the womb
against a tired uterus;
he runs the obstacle race
of infant mortality,
arriving at the battle ground
of the six killer diseases.

He trains in the athletic
field of hunger, winning
protein and calorie races
of kwashiorkor and marasmus.

He is a champ, yet to
hold a world title
against modernity, democracy
and   sophistication, which breed
in favour of war and bloodshed.

He is a third world champion.

The Vase

The vase, which my husband got me
for my birthday
has a rose-eyed base;
it sits making a statement.

A Dark Night

A tunnel of months frozen together
in mean darkness that threatens
to attack: darkness becomes a cover
as I lie under the night sky,
wanting to find meaning
on our sacramental bed.

I stay alone in the darkness,
on this passage of time,
which flies as if it
is mercy's way of keeping me
safe from the night's daggers.

I am living at the heart of time:
it is darkest but also the quietest.
All creation seems to have slept,
thieves roam   breaking into
people's homes.

On this landscape of time,
three dogs walk gently
on the dark path towards me:
we sit quietly together on the

cold cemented floor, breathing
the same air; the dogs,
the silence and I.

We watch the winds of time roll
from the deepest dawn
to soft pink light of the morning.
With it, comes a gentle voice:
"Do as I would do."

Celebration

My home,
a fighting arena;
children scream
to win a *mweso* game.

A sickbay,
hot foreheads,
red eyes,
blocked noses,
rebelling stomachs.

I touch sorrow,
tasting defeat.

Later, at a refugee camp,
I bend inside a pot,
look   up in each
begging eye, wondering
whom to favour.

I am asked:
– *Why produce so many children?* –
What is too many children?

Does a mother know?

My answer comes easily:
I celebrate children
amidst poverty.

Shoreline

The storms have passed,
the tides have left;
the ocean floor is covered
with clean white sand;
debris   lines the fringes,
the skyline is clearing
of moody clouds.

Walking here today,
many things distract my eyes:
if I am careful, I can select
pebbles from the mud.

With care, I treasure these items,
each showing effects of the storm.

Hanging Threads

Mother is shadowed by light:
a grand homecoming,
a marriage of her own
in a few weeks.

She who is the first comes last
to become a young star
in *Nakazi* sky.

Our family knits
delicate threads, loosely
hanging.

A sibling clash can leave a
torn parch, but a day doesn't
end before we tie each thread by
candlelight, till   dawn is a
clear sky in our hearts.

Her grandchildren see the invisible
cord, which tangles around all
of them and from one womb,

which is stronger than death,
lighting journeys of each soul.

A Poem on a Bus

A bus journey isn't
ordinary.

It is a stretch of landscape
in the memories of my innards,
travelling with me.

A bus journey is
an unravelling of a dull pain
hidden somewhere in the
vessels beneath my chest.

A bus journey is
a long road to safety,
happening when I distance
myself from what
lies at the heart of things.

A bus journey is
a spiritual spiral of the mind
winding and untying to
freedom, a time to
find some solace

among strangers:
us being alone together.

It is a burrowing
through a tunnel
of answers lingering
at every corner,
voices whispering that life
is difficult yet the solution
is within me.

To have the ability to travel
far in my imagination,
the bus takes me to that
place which exists only to
myself and my being.

A bus journey is
a spiritual spiral of the mind
winding and unwinding
to freedom; a time to
find truth among the strange.

My child sees

My child sees,
my child feels:
her body is young,
her soul is bottomless.

She says it is good
to cry, sharing her
gift with me.

When my syllables lie under
a heavy tongue, hers
bounce up and down,
slide left and right,
weaving stories of play.

Cooking for a son

When I visit my son,
I cook,
I clear cobwebs,
preparing for
nurturing relationships
in his life.

In his space
as a mother I pray,
drawing God close.

Acorn of my tree

I just love plants,
I should have become a botanist;
but may be I could have turned
it into an academic endeavour,
not a pleasurable one   I now enjoy.

My Coma Tale

They tell me I was at
death's jaws, being pierced
by its arrows on a hospital bed
in my village.

They prayed for my soul, hoping
I was talking to angels or
sitting on Jesus's lap, but I was on
urgent business.

I jumped out of the window
to land on a mat of grass below;
I had things to buy in the market:
things like needles and match boxes;
I ran most of the way, hitting
my toes on stones, falling, bleeding.

My throat was dry, I needed a drink;
then I came back home
to wake up and find members of
my family crying. I asked,
Who is sick?

A Fertile Desert

You are tending a desert,
it is fertile;
what do you feed it?
What is its name?

Higenyi

In memory of Higenyi, the student journalist who was shot by the police on 12th January 2002.

I watched the grass shake
off the dew in young sunlight,
I watched a hen cluck
its hunting song.

I watched the taxi driver
calling passengers as he yawned,
I watched the town fill with people
gathering for a rally.

I watched policemen
resembling beetles
take cover,
I heard the crack of gunfire.

I watched someone fall
like a cut banana stem,
clad in a blue jacket and
white socks; his blood
pooled on the road,

drowning his body.

I thought I watched his
dream die, not making it
to report the news;
I was wrong:
he was the news.

A Sketch

An artist trusts a pencil's nib, the nib
knows not where the circle begins
and ends; but if it stays on its
sharpened tip long enough,
a form emerges.

My pen knows not what word
will be the child of its ink,
but if it trusts my leading,
the ink weaves a story about
its beginning; a beginning when
the page was blank because
there was nothing to darken it.

Every human being is an incomplete
sketch, drifting in life's currents,
to farther worlds, leaving behind
the point of the pen in themselves.

A Bee-kissed Garden

Your garden sends eternal smiles:
I throw up my hands in surrender,
its soul is delicate, soft and
colourful.

Your garden receives visitors;
your lavender is a bee-kissed purple.

Thank you for sharing your
garden with me.

Something vulnerable

Endiro ushers in my friend Angela:
a big girl with fresh looking features,
wears no bra, and unconscious of it.

I could never have guessed her age
until she tells me she is learning
to face the grief of not bearing children:
she just turned forty without hope
of meeting the right man;
Angela's dream was to become
a mother and a queen.

Across the road I meet another
self-oblivious woman: her breasts hang
loosely on her bare chest,
she is half naked.

Her features charred charcoal-black
by the sun, she dangles on unsteady feet,
she attracts everyone's attention for
the unsteadiness, for walking naked
on the street, for being unwell.

Whereas Angela is approached for attractiveness,
this woman is avoided for her lunacy:
her unsteadiness is vulnerable,
pitiable.

She walks nowhere and everywhere
with a hand beating lightly at her breast:
she is a woman who needs a touch, yet
the passer-bys look on at her wandering feet
as she walks in her darkened shadow.

It is pity that draws me to her; I gave her
some shillings, she takes the note from me
quietly, heading her way.

A few steps away from her, I look back
and watch her walk barefooted
on her relentless journey with her shoulders
beaten by the sun; I feel a tenderness
for her restlessness.

In the same town a few blocks ahead,
a man carries his wife on a *boda boda*,
holding her the way a mother holds
a six-months-old baby on her lap;
he carries her gently   hugged in his chest.

Spider

Do not waste precious silk,
little spider;
borrow the wings of a bird
and fly to freedom.

Candle

Candle: in your flame I see
an ice-cream cone;
a delicate base and a yellow top.

Candle: your red–hot wick
endures the burning; you are cleverly
hiding the black soot in the flame,
yet your wax is melting, rolling,
like tears   pooling at the base,
forming a white pavement.

Meeting as Spirit

I want to meet as spirit
so that I can touch the
faraway friend to come near.

I want to meet as spirit
so that tenderness
becomes touchable, and
I can give and receive.

I want to meet as spirit
so that goodness as an
unspoken word
wins on my lips.

I want to meet as spirit
so that I am spirit,
spirit is me
and spirit is us.

My flower's path

This plant pours itself inside out:
I am healed by the freshness of its look,
softened by the smoothness of its petals,
brightened by the colour of its skin;
there is purity in its core.

I too can become a living flower
propped inside out of the earth.

Little Edens

If you asked me about the value
of your garden, I would say,
is it the time collected in the flower pots.

The smell of my flowering jasmine
and lavender, with frogs croaking in
the background is my ideal.

My garden and I are maturing together;
it is a small land, but I have made it
my own little Eden.

In life we must find little things which
give us pleasure: we choose our own
happiness in whatever form it takes;
we cultivate our own little Edens.

Falling

The rain is gently clapping
at the rocks outside my kitchen,
its music waters my desert.

A new song forms,
the sounds of raindrops
on my face.

The rain is steadily
taking me home
by twilight.

I am learning from the weeping clouds
that falling isn't dying.

www.ingramcontent.com/pod-product-compliance
Lightning Source LLC
Chambersburg PA
CBHW020626300426
44113CB00007B/788